Social Competence: reading other people

Dr Gerald Lombard

Social Competence: reading other people

Published by Lifetime Careers Wiltshire, 7 Ascot Court, White Horse Business Park, Trowbridge BA14 0XA.

ISBN 1 902876 69 5

Printed by Cromwell Press, Trowbridge
Cover illustration by Russell Cobb
Text design by Ministry of Design

Motivating the Disaffected

Series editor: Dr Gerald Lombard

Social Competence: reading other people is one of a series of six titles designed to help professionals in education and advisory work to motivate and encourage students who are disengaged from learning.

Each book provides a concise and practical guide to topics that are of particular concern to teachers and advisers.

The other titles in the series are:

The ABC Approach to Classroom Behaviour Management
Asperger Syndrome and high fuctioning autism:
          guidelines for education post 16
Complex Specific Learning Difficulties
Motivational Triggers
Staying Safe

To order copies, please contact Orca Book Services Ltd, Stanley House, 3 Fleets Lane, Poole, Dorset BH15 3AJ. Tel: 01202 665432. Fax: 01202 666219.

For further information about these and other products published by Lifetime Careers Publishing, please contact our customer services, tel: 01225 716023; email: sales@lifetime-publishing.co.uk, or www.lifetime-publishing.co.uk

Dr Gerald Lombard, C. Psychol., AFBPsS

Ged is Director of The Independent Psychological Service, which is an
intervention and training service for young people and adults. He primarily
works with individuals who 'won't, can't or can't be arsed' (one client's view
of their work).

As a Chartered Psychologist, his major areas of interest are motivational
principles, social competency (reading faces with intent) and complex specific
learning difficulties. Ged was a secondary school teacher for 15 years, a part-
time tutor/psychologist at two prisons and has held his current post for ten
years.

Contents

Introduction

The modern study of social competence gained vigour in the 1950s and 1960s with findings that correlated social competence and mental health (Dodge *et al.,* 1989). Farrington (1991) added weight to growing evidence that social incompetence and antisocial behaviour in early and middle childhood were two predictors of antisocial personality in adulthood.

Social competence has had varied interpretations over the years: some theorists thought of it as a personality trait, whereas others conceptualised competence as a series of skills. Indeed, it was Michael Argyle who invented the concept of social skills (Lamb and Joshi, 2002): in his view, social skills are similar to manual or other motor skills. They can therefore be taught through training or other demonstration, and learned through practice and feedback. A commonly accepted definition of social competence is: the ability to attain personal goals in social situations (Lombard, 1992; Lombard and Bigglestone, 2002).

Training programmes have been created for people who are shy or suffering from minor mental problems, acknowledging that lack of social competence might exacerbate these conditions. Researchers and practitioners have used such training with troubled adolescents to help them to control their antisocial behaviour, and with violent offenders to help them to manage their own anger and aggression. It has often remained fixed in the areas of clinical research and practice, or in custodial settings.

This type of training is now commonplace in everyday working life, e.g. training staff in service industries, police training, training of healthcare professionals, and now to improve doctors' communication skills. However, social competency training remains an unidentified flying object at various levels of education, youth training and youth justice. For example, in a review of education and training methods offered to vulnerable and challenging young people (Lombard and Bigglestone, 2002, 2003), only 15% of training providers and colleges in some regions (e.g. South Wales and Lancashire) were able to explain adequately what was meant by social competency training, soft skills training or social skills training. Responses varied from 'helping with housing', 'we don't really know' to 'whether they have progressed as an individual to where they function as a positive element of society.' There was little evidence of reliable or valid assessments to determine the social competency levels of young people. Of more concern, there were very few examples of planned, and graduated courses for social competency acquisition.

So why is it important to learn this type of competence? Nowicki* in his research of social and personal skills in three countries (USA, Australia and England), concluded that 10% of individuals have a non-verbal reading deficit, i.e. one in ten individuals have difficulty interpreting a face or tone of voice expression on one of four basic core emotions (happy, sad, anger or fear). However, he has demonstrated that the level of non-verbal deficit can be assessed and remediated (Nowicki and Duke, 2002). He has used a term called 'dyssemia' to describe the inability of this group to understand and follow the unwritten rules of non-verbal communication. Individuals who would meet the 'dyssemic' criteria would be those who:

- continue with an action/activity even when it leads to punishment

- lack social maturity

- have difficulty recognising a dangerous situation

- have difficulty understanding rules

- often feel sad, lonely, bewildered, confused and anxious.

Nowicki emphasises that awareness is the key. Many practitioners and parents fail to recognise the problems, and subsequently individuals are ostracised and excluded without ever knowing why. The DANVA2 (Nowicki and Duke, 2002) is a diagnostic analysis on CD-ROM that can both assess and help remediate this type of difficulty.

* from personal conversations with the author; publication pending

The extent of the need

My work takes me across counties in England, Wales and Northern Ireland. Although my direct intervention work with young people and adults is situated in Wiltshire and Swindon, I frequently hear professionals in education, training and youth justice requesting information and resources for helping individuals' personal and social development. Basic skills training in numeracy, literacy and information technology can only do so much. Finding the appropriate level of training or employment helps motivate, but when essential 'people skills' are missing, then someone's future in a chosen area may be short-lived. I see this occurring more often now than before, and I hear professional colleagues around the UK expressing the same. Our regional research work has observed it, Nowicki's international studies confirm it, and my daily intervention work certainly keeps me busy with it! So why has it happened? Why have such a large proportion of individuals failed to acquire basic social competencies to navigate their way around human relationships at school, college, training, the workplace?

David Moore, one of Her Majesty's Inspector of Schools, has provided an explanation that neatly summarises what we know through research, and what our everyday experience is showing us. It is called the Circles of Social Participation (see Diagram 1 overleaf).

Circle of intimacy

I was born into a family in the North-east of England, and had a mother, father, brother and sister in my circle of intimacy. My brother was ten years older than me, my sister 14 years older than me. Our family had a large extended network both where we lived and in Ireland. By the age of four, I had already been taught to read faces by my intimacy circle. For example, when I saw kindly Uncle Kelly coming down the garden path with a big cheery smile and a slightly wobbly gait, I would perch myself on his knee

Diagram 1: The circles of social participation

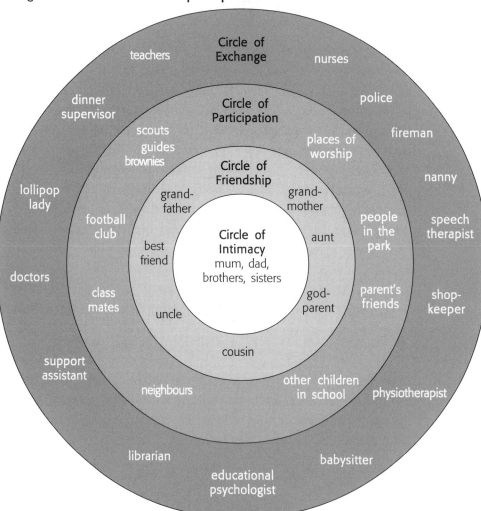

when he sat on the sofa, give him a kiss on his cheek, and duly receive a Mars bar or half a crown (12½ pence). If Nan entered the house with a slow step, her beautiful steel blue eyes looking around, then I was off – because she would look at the back of my neck, and if it was dirty she would scrub it with a flannel and Vim. If she entered the house swiftly, with a fleeting smile, then I would hang around for a custard cream biscuit.

Circle of friendship

There were cousins, aunties, uncles and family friends – the circle of friendship. There were lots of people entering the house, and relatives advising me about a moody auntie, a cheeky cousin, and telling me to watch out when he/she looks at you 'this way' because 'you'll be in for it', or 'don't sit like that/talk like that' in front of that posh uncle and auntie. My brother brought to the house what I remember as hairy, testosterone-driven friends whom I behaved differently with than with my sister's friends – they were gentler, sat differently, looked and spoke softly. Yet despite their gender differences, and variety of ways of communication, they all wanted me upstairs, out of the way, and asleep by 9 pm! However, I learned a great deal from this wave of human communication coming into and leaving the house. Of course, we also visited these people in their own houses, and met other people I had seen before. There was lots to learn and remember, and if I did not learn quickly enough, there was always someone ready to advise me.

This experience is very different from the situation in many households today. Some relationships founder when a child is very young, a new partner is found, and perhaps another sibling arrives with that new partner. The new relationship may also falter, so that each family break-up results in one or both adults, with their children, living in different places. Network ties with any extended family may be broken, neighbours are strangers and fewer people visit the new family home. The little four-year-old has a restricted diet of social exchange with only a few different adults. New visitors may not be consistent visitors. So, when the four-year-old asks his father for help when playing with toys on the table, he only has very restricted options from which to choose, e.g. *'Dad, Dad, help me here, now'* – because he has not learned the different ways of reading other people's responses, or learned alternative methods of asking for help in different situations. So, perhaps, the first expression he sees on a teacher's face is one of straight-faced irritation for a rude and clumsy way of asking for help – but that child may not have learned an alternative. Further, his restricted repertoire of how to behave with his peers may isolate him socially.

The Family Conference in London in 2001 also expressed key issues related to the healthy maintenance of young children. For example, independent carers for very young children of working parents may provide food, warmth and safety but the absence of a thriving, busy life of a household with relations and visitors may hinder the essential exchanges and social learning within and beyond the family. Indeed, sitting with a parent at least once a day, and eating together, was seen as one of several essential elements in the healthy development of young people.

Circle of participation

Communicating with local people and peers (neighbours, postman, classmates, friends at clubs or church) would be included in this circle of participation. However, many of these relationships are now tenuous: because of more frequent moving and loss of kinship networks there is less neighbourliness (I could be two miles from my home on the estate I lived on in the North-east and someone could ask: *'Hey, Gerald, does your mother know you are down here?'*); classmates have more relationship difficulties resulting in increased confrontations, often because they cannot read the intention of another peer; there is less acceptance of business callers to the house – even postmen and women have less constant customers to chat to; attendances at clubs – such as cubs, brownies, guides, scouts, youth clubs, sports teams, etc – have declined as more young people have increased interest in more isolated pursuits; church attendances have continued to drop and with it other group activities that were related to church attendance; and community centres are less likely to be used for informal group purposes (bingo, quiz nights, dances) than they used to be – instead, large, anonymous groups of people meet together in bars and clubs in towns and cities.

Children are less likely to play on the street or on playing fields or in parks. They are less likely to talk to strangers. Parents are more inclined to keep children in the safety of their own homes, often based on exaggerated fears of abduction. Often, parents prefer their children to amuse themselves with the TV, videos, CDs, computers and DVDs rather than run the risk of meeting 'undesirables'. It is almost a case of turning away from people, their faces, the social exchange – a perverse way of staying safe by failing to learn the essential skills of social survival. Research continues to confirm that many social phobias are related to weak social skills and limited social competencies. We may be creating fear and anxiety by trying to protect our children from it. Perhaps we could best serve children by teaching them the social and personal skills with which to cope.

Circle of exchange

This outer circle is where we enter society and use the social competencies we have learned, or struggle to make sense of what is happening around us, and to us. So, those individuals who have not gained a repertoire of responses by understanding others' social signals will appear gauche, or aggressive, or gawky, or withdrawn.

Hence, some people do not know how to talk to teachers, nurses, doctors – they speak to them (or demand service) in the only restricted ways that they have learned or witnessed. Some individuals have not learned the best way to speak to the police and thus increase their likelihood of being charged. A former client (Paul) was stopped by police while driving in the wrong lane into Bristol – the police officer was only attempting to advise him as a visitor about which lanes were now being used for quick routes into the city. The resulting slanging match occurred because Paul began the conversation with the officer: *'You can't have stopped me for speeding, I wasn't speeding,'* – 'No, sir,' – *'You can't stop me for faulty lights, I've checked them,'* – 'No, sir' – *'What the **** have you stopped me for?'* – 'For being in the two-plus lane, sir' – *'What the **** is the two-******* lane?'.*

Paul was arrested, and his car impounded. He was surprised to learn that a smile, good eye contact and a simple *'Yes, officer'* would have been all that was required to enable him to quickly continue his journey to Bristol.

To include social competency training in our educational programmes and training schemes – as early as possible – could help alleviate many of the problems our young people face. If they cannot interpret other people's intent, they will always assume the worst, i.e. 'I do not know what you are likely to be thinking, but it is probably not very nice about me, so I will get the first strike in'. This is sometimes referred to as developing a 'Theory of Nasty Mind'.

These competencies are teachable. We need to start making a start in the mainstream to help this group – and not wait until they are referred for clinical, psychological or custodial treatment.

However, arguments abound as to whose responsibility it is. As I sit writing these words, there below the banner headline 'Ofsted head says that five-year-olds have led disrupted and dishevelled lives'. It is a lead article in *The Sunday Telegraph* of 31 August 2003 in which David Bell (head of Ofsted) says one of the key causes of language difficulties in schools is the failure of parents to impose proper discipline at home, which leads to poor behaviour in the classroom. Another serious concern expressed was the tendency to sit children in front of the TV, rather than talking and playing with them, resulting in many children being unable to communicate effectively when they start school. Bell, and headteachers, go on to say that many children start school with minimal social skills – because *'many children have never sat at a table because their parents let them eat their tea sitting on the floor (not communicating) in front of the TV'*. It goes on to say, quoting the General Secretary of the National Association of Head Teachers, that *'these parents are giving their children a raw deal'*.

Well, who can argue with that? My contention is that we have known this for well over ten years – look at the dates quoted of the research in the Appendix of this book, many are over ten years old. However, education has been – for well over ten years – unhealthily focused on basic academic skills targets, and now we are entering the second generation of children with very weak social competency skills.

Rather than apportioning blame, the necessary building blocks should be being put in place for a very large number of young people who *do not know* they have communication difficulties – how can they when they do not learn how to communicate from their parents? Unless addressed, we will have a third generation of parents without the communication skills to teach their children.

Therefore, the problem is extensive, it is growing, and it remains generally unaddressed. Hence my proposal that the area of social competency is brought into mainstream teaching and education in general.

Section 1
Is social competence related to specific difficulties?

Learning disabilities

An increasing number of studies have suggested that children with learning disabilities are less skilled in interpreting facial expression than normally achieving peers (Whiting and Robinson, 2002). Whiting and Robinson's work supported claims by Dimitrovski *et al.,* (1998) and Rourke and Fuerst (1991), that young people with visual processing types of learning difficulties are more likely to have problems with interpretation of subtle visual cues critical to understanding social events. This can exist despite supportive and effective parenting.

Therefore, socially incompetent young people may selectively attend to negative cues more than their peers, leading to negative views about social interaction (Crick and Dodge, 1994). However, the usual diagnostic batteries for learning disabilities do not include assessments of social competence. To limit assessment of learning problems to difficulties in literacy, numeracy and IT ignores the importance of social interactions, reducing the possibility that we will help young people effectively or help them fully understand the nature of their problems (Whiting and Robinson, 2002). Intervention programmes for such young people usually concentrate on academic skill building rather than on the development of social competencies (Lombard and Bigglestone, 2003), and yet longitudinal evidence suggests a link between significant social and workplace problems in later life and social adjustment in childhood and teenage years (Parker and Asher, 1987).

There does appear to be a need for a coordinated approach that reflects a wider menu for a young person's presenting needs, including the promotion of social skills and the understanding of cues of social interaction. This approach could include teaching young people how to express their own feelings and how to interpret the expressions and emotions of other people, with the hope that enabling broader communication skills will help develop social competence, improve self-esteem and reduce problem behaviour (Whiting and Robinson, 2002). Such approaches would require the training of teachers and support workers so that they are appropriately prepared to address and teach the skills required.

ADD/ADHD

Problems with social interaction have also been identified in a sub-group of children with Attention Deficit Disorder (ADD)/Attention Deficit Hyperactivity Disorder (ADHD). Kinsbourne (1991) identified a sub-group whom he called 'overfocused' because they became 'stuck' on certain activities. Among the characteristics he identified for this group was a difficulty reading non-verbal cues such as facial expressions. Nowicki* described this in more detail: he referred to it as a 'systematic' non-verbal deficit, which resulted in a failure of reading one non-verbal system, such as the face, or the tone of voice, or gestures, or posture. Tracey and Gleeson (1998) found teenagers with ADHD reported significantly less concern about others' feelings, and about relationships with others, than did non-ADHD teenagers.

Scotopic Sensitivity Syndrome (SSS)

This is a visual perceptual dysfunction, which has also been linked with non-verbal processing deficit. Individuals with SSS report a shadowing and doubling of letters and words while reading, as well as blurring and movement of print and a reduced span of focus (Irlen, 1991). Such distortions may be generalised as the misperception of subtle differences in facial expression and

* from personal conversations with the author; publication pending

body language (Stafford and Grosser, 1993). Studies have found (Whiting and Robinson, 2002) that intervention by the application of specifically tinted coloured lenses to modify some young peoples' visual perception resulted in a change in ability to recognise faces, and facial emotion.

Dyslexia

There are a large number of studies and texts indicating that a significant proportion of individuals with specific learning difficulties/dyslexia (SpLD/Dyslexia) experience social problems and emotional difficulties (Kuhne and Weiner, 2000; Fawcett, 2001). Often, this is attributed to failure within the educational system, or an individual's disaffection with restricted future options. Although this is likely to play a part for some groups of individuals, there is evidence of sub-types within SpLD/Dyslexia that may be less skilled than achieving peers in making social inferences and reading small changes in facial expression (Bruno, 1981; Crick and Dodge, 1994). Although this does not seem related to visual processing of social cues (Whiting and Robinson, 2002), it may be related to the time it takes to process the information (Fawcett, 2001). In other words, results that indicate slower reading of facial expression than their non-dyslexic peers, may relate to dyslexics' apparent difficulty with speeded and automatic tasks, including picture naming.

Autism spectrum disorders

In the 1980s, the social impairment of individuals labelled autistic was thought to be a failure to recognise emotion in others. However, this failure to recognise emotion in others was found to be not only specific to autism. Baron-Cohen (1989), and Baron-Cohen and Joliffe (1997) proposed a deficit of social cognition, or theory of mind – an individual being unable to 'put themselves in someone else's shoes'. Although a substantial proportion

(80%) of Baron-Cohen's autistic group were unable to read what others may be thinking, one of his diagnostic procedures (e.g. reading another's eye expression) helped to show how non-autistics could also have difficulties reading eyes (Lombard *et al.*, 2003).

Happé (1999) concluded that individuals with autism have a specific cognitive style, rather than a series of deficits. For example, children with autism are thought to process faces in terms of individual features, not their overall expression – indeed, they suffer fewer problems in face recognition tests when faces are inverted (Hobson *et al.*, 1988). Several studies (Piven *et al.*, 1995) have found that some people with autism have larger or heavier brains than do comparison groups, with increased cell density in certain areas. It is possible that increased cell density reflects an abnormal increase in the number of neurons. This may be due to failure of 'neuron pruning' in brain development (Happé, 1999), resulting in processing information with excess neurons. By so doing, there may be a failure to gain the 'gist' (overall, salient points) of information – in other words, if the brain has the capacity to encode and decode each separate event or individual expression it encounters, perhaps there is not a need for the economy of 'only' gaining the gist of an expression.

Therefore, it is possible that autism may result from an excess of riches at the neurological level. This may result in a cognitive system too able to deal with the bigger picture of facial expression and other aspects within the visual, cognitive and neural world.

Pemberton (1999) reported a case study of a child with autism who had significant improvements in social interaction as a consequence of the use of coloured lens filters. There is further research ongoing that is examining the possible overlap between Irlen Syndrome and autism.

Section 2
The language of social competence

For an understanding of social competence, both non-verbal communication and verbal communication should be considered.

Therefore, I will outline what I see as the two key channels of both aspects of communication, in the context of teaching more effective social competencies. Each competency will have some suggested teaching methods to follow. These will include ice-breakers as well as exercises. Any ice-breaker or exercise should have explanations to follow from the trainer to the learner and, again, some of these will be included.

Facial expression

There are two processes in facial communication: expressive and receptive, i.e. sending our feelings to others, and reading the feelings of others. Social competency problems (social incompetence) are frequently related to difficulties with making eye contact. Numerous studies have confirmed that effective eye contact and appropriate smiling are the two most frequently noted characteristics of children and young adults.

During a conversation, we spend 30-60% of the time looking at the other person's face. If we do not look at them for at least that proportion of time, we are losing essential interpersonal information about them. However, even with adequate eye contact, the individual may not be able to read another's facial expression. Nowicki and Duke (1992) identified 'happiness' as the most easily identified emotion, but that sadness, anger and fear are more difficult to read as facial expressions of emotion, e.g. a sad face may be read as an angry face, resulting in ignoring or avoidance as opposed to a caring response.

Sometimes the facial expression is lost completely from interpretation, and is sometimes threateningly followed with *'What are you looking at?'*.

Reading faces is one side, sending facial expressions that express our emotions is another. Many young people send facial expressions that they do not intend, or at the wrong intensity. Often, awareness then practice can alleviate some of these problem. Nowicki's findings indicate that between 7% and 10% of young people have significant difficulty in either reading or producing specific emotional expressions. This group are prone to be disliked by their peers, and more likely to be unhappy.

Guidelines for helping young people develop better facial communication skills

- Assess level of eye-reading skills: develop your own booklet of eye expressions, e.g. photographs of eyes-only expressions, with two or three options available of what the eyes are expressing (sad, surprised, happy). One of our booklets with 30 sets of eyes expect 20 out of 30 correct for reasonable reading of eyes, 25 out of 30 for good reading of eyes, and above 25 out of 30 for accurate reading of eyes. (Eye test available from Wakefield Publications – see contact details listed in the Appendix.)

- Assess face reading skills (Nowicki and Duke, 2002; Baron-Cohen and Joliffe, 1997).

- Develop a pictionary of eye expressions and facial expressions. Add new ones as you find them.

- Make a pack of cards with eyes or face on one side, and the correct answer on the other side of the card.

- Play a form of charades with each other, using facial expressions.

- Show a facial expression (e.g. happy face) and ask the learner how a particular sentence would be said with specific facial expressions, e.g. *'I want to leave now.'*

- Play eye-contact games, such as those described overleaf.

Game 1 – The looking game

Ask individuals to sit opposite each other in pairs, with knees/faces opposite each other, looking at each other's faces, without a table/obstacle between them. Allow them to giggle, talk, shout, laugh – but eventually (after one or two minutes) ask for quiet, and ask them what you had requested. Someone is likely to say *'You asked us to sit opposite each other and look at one another'*. You can respond with *'But what you did was talk, giggle, laugh, shout – but all I want you to do is look at each other, not talk, giggle or laugh, this is a serious exercise – now look at each other'*. Chaos may ensue, and then you ask them more pleadingly to look at each other and not laugh, giggle or talk – but the more you ask the more they often laugh, giggle or talk (a major part of doing the exercise, which shows why looking at someone aids communication!).

Eventually, it should settle down a little; ask one of the pair to raise one hand in the air while still looking at the partner. (You may wish to chastise one or two people by saying, *'Don't look at me, look at him/her'* or *'Stop giggling/talking – this is a serious exercise!'*.) Then ask the person who put their hand up to put their hand down, keep looking at their partner, and say to them *'I love you.'* This is likely to create more pandemonium. Wait for people to express their love. Once order is eventually maintained, ask the person who hasn't yet raised their hand to do so now (more chastisement from you, the degree of which depends on the make-up of your group). Ask them to keep looking at each other. The last person to have raised their hand is now asked to say: *'I love you, too'* to their partner – again wait for them to carry out your instruction!

This game may not be appropriate for some groups and individuals. However, it is intended to be a fun, sometimes chaotic, exercise, with the intention of highlighting eye contact as a source of enjoyable communication. The way the game is explained is crucial. Suggestions are made after game 6.

Game 2 – Killer-wink

Each person receives a card face down, all except one card is blank – the exceptional card has a cross on it. No one is to see another's card, nor let anyone see their card. The person with the card with the cross is now 'The Killer'. Before dealing the cards, the explanation of the game is:

'I want us all to sit so we can see each others' faces. Each person will receive a card. The person who receives the card with the 'X' marked on it is the killer. Do not let anyone see your card, or know what was on your card (best avoided by collecting all cards in when everybody has had a glance at their card). *The killer kills people by winking at them. When you see someone wink at you, you die – dying can be quiet, such as a final dying breath, and sitting with you arms folded, or spectacular, such as a Bonny and Clyde shoot-out. Don't die as soon as you see someone wink at you – it makes it too easy to guess who is the killer. If you see someone wink at another person, then you can report the killer to me, by putting your hand in the air or saying to me 'I know the killer.' When I say 'Who is it?', if you point to the person who admits they are the killer, then the killer dies and you stay alive, and win the game. If you point to the person who says they are not the killer you die, and the person you wrongly accused dies with you. So be careful before you accuse! OK, game on, no talking, and all look at each others' faces.'*

You may want to have more than one killer to spice up the game – or give everybody blank cards and be the killer yourself (a distinct advantage because you can kill your accusers as they look at you!).

Again, chaos may ensue – but the overall aim of the game is to get people looking at each other, having fun, and hopefully giggling at the madness of it all.

Game 3 – Mushy peas

Three or four chairs are placed at the front of the room, with the group facing the chairs. Your instructions to the group are: *'This is a simple game. All I want is three/four people to sit at the front on the chairs* (point to your selected persons, or you may have volunteers). *Now the rules are...* (you may then start sending people back to their places if they sit and smile, or do not look at you, or speak – this may go on for some time, i.e. people going backwards and forwards from the chairs at the front – eventually say)... *we must get on with this .... the rules are: rule one – you are to look at me; rule two – you are not to smile*, (if anyone does not look at you or they smile, you send them back to their place and someone else takes their place); *and rule three – if I ask you any question, you answer with the words 'mushy peas' – do you understand?'.* (If anyone says *'Yes'* or doesn't answer, they go back to their place for not answering the question with *'mushy peas.'*)

The object of the game – again – is to get people to giggle and laugh, while looking at your face. You can add questions that may aid giggling: *'What did you wash your face in this morning?', 'What is in your knickers/underpants?'* etc.

Game 4 – The face game

This is an activity that could be used with any age group. It will encourage the understanding and development of social skills and competencies in 'reading' facial expressions and non-verbal communication. It is also an activity that can be used to develop communication skills.

Resources

- Large sheets of flip chart paper prepared with pictures of faces from magazines stuck on them. You will need a selection of old/young; male/female, etc.

- Number each one for identification purposes.

- Large sheet of flip chart paper with the questions on and plain paper for people to record their answers on.

Or

- A4 sheet with the questions on and space for everyone to record their answers. You will need one sheet per person.

Organisation

- Pin up the sheets with the faces on and the sheet with the questions on. (It will depend on the size of the group as to whether one large question sheet is the most appropriate way.)

- Give out either the A4 question sheets *or* the plain paper.

- People individually look at the faces and record the number against each question of the face they feel best answers that question for them.

- No discussion or conferring!

- Set a time limit for doing this part of the activity.

- In groups of two, share answers and encourage students to say why they made their choices.

- As a group/class, collate answers, seek explanations for choices, etc.

Game 5 – Portrait gallery

This activity is designed to encourage people to communicate in various ways – visually, verbally, physically.

Resources

- Pieces of paper to be prepared beforehand with the name of a person written on it at the top that corresponds to the name of someone in the group.

- Everyone to be given at least one piece of paper each.

- One or more large sheet/s of flip chart paper prepared beforehand, which is divided up into 'squares' – one for each person in the group.

Organisation

- Everyone has to go round the rest of the group and introduce themselves and say one positive thing about themselves, e.g. what they like to do as a hobby, something they are good at, etc.

- They look for the person whose name is on their piece of paper *but* they must not tell that person they are looking for them.

- After a period of time (check everyone has met 'their' person) they then have to draw a picture of that person.

- Folding the name of the person over so that the rest of the group cannot see it, each person in turn holds their picture up and the rest of the group has to guess who it is in the group. Much hilarity will ensue!

- When it has been guessed the picture is stuck on the prepared portrait gallery sheet.

- The game will allow each person to meet, communicate verbally and physically (via handshake), etc.

- When they are drawing the person eye contact will be encouraged as it will be when the pictures are being shown.

Game 6 - What's my job?

This is an activity that will encourage people to 'look up' at people's faces, to develop communication skills and to develop some understanding of jobs.

Resources

- Write jobs or whatever on 'post-its' or stickers – at least one per person. (Depending on the group/individuals you may need to be sensitive as to where the post-it is stuck!) A fun alternative could be to have the names of animals, pop stars, etc.

- Split the group into two groups – A and B.

- Stick a 'post-it' on the forehead of each person so that other people can see the job written on it but not the person on whom it is stuck. An alternative could be to make 'crowns' with the jobs written on or have pieces of card with string/elastic to fit round the head.

Organisation

- The task is for each person to find out what their job is.

- Group A start and they can ask one question only to each person in group B. The questions must be asked in such a way that they can be answered with a 'yes' or 'no'.

- If someone guesses their job they can be given another one.

- Swap the groups over after a set period of time so that group B has to guess their jobs.

- A checklist of questions might need to be prepared for use, depending on the ability of the group.

- Group discussion, when the activity has been completed, could include such questions as: *'Which questions were the most useful/least useful?'*; *'How did you go about narrowing down the possibilities?'*; *'Do they know anything about their job?'*, etc.

As with all games, you need to choose your time and choose your group. However, it essential to explain why you are playing these games, i.e. explain the importance of looking at someone's face when they are speaking. Unless we do so, we are likely to miss important information they are conveying to us.

This may not only mean interpersonal information conveyed through non-verbal communication but it can also result in missing key items of information contained in the verbal message. Campbell, in her work on lipreading, used the 'McGurk Effect' to demonstrate the importance of looking at someone's face when they are talking. She was able to demonstrate how, when someone was looking at another when they spoke, the auditory cortex received an increase in blood flow and signal output, compared to less activity when they listened but did not look, i.e. the auditory (listening part of the brain) 'lit up' when looking at someone's face while they spoke.

However, a more impressive demonstration was one I experienced during one of Professor Campbell's talks at the University of York in 1999, attended by dozens of psychologists. She asked the audience to look at a still picture of Professor McGurk on the projector screen. All duly did, and being cynical psychologists, we awaited to be marginally impressed by some type of illusion. Campbell asked us to write down the three words we were to hear McGurk speak. Pens and paper at the ready, McGurk looked at us and we all 'heard' him say 'car', 'wha' and 'har'. At least that is what we all wrote, and all agreed we heard him say.

Campbell then asked us to listen to the same soundtrack, but this time there was no moving face of McGurk on the screen – only a blank screen. The soundtrack we listened to a second time clearly said 'a' 'a' and 'a' (the 'a' sound as in apple). In other words, the soundtrack only said the same three phonic units, yet we had all 'heard' the words uttered from his lips as 'car', 'wha' and 'har'. Why was this?

McGurk had actually only mouthed 'car', 'wha' and 'har' but no sound came from his lips. His mouth shape for each 'utterence' was synchronised with the phonic sounds 'a', 'a' and 'a'. In other words, a silent McGurk moving his mouth, and the same three phonic sounds – combined – gave us an illusion of hearing words that were not actually spoken or said.

The implication of this type of effect is far reaching, not only in terms of Campbell's work on lipreading but also in how it demonstrates the way we interpret information. By looking at someone's face while they speak, we are quickly formulating 3D images of what is being sent to us. By listening only to the sounds, it becomes a weaker 2D communication.

For me, and dozens of other psychologists watching and listening that day, we quickly understood the consequences of looking and listening ... and appreciated how an effective lip-reader can 'hear' a lot more in human communication than they are often credited with. Indeed, a colleague was recently telling me that his partner (a highly proficient lip-reader with partial hearing) often gets embarrassed at parties and social gatherings – because she can read what others believe is whispered or private information!

Therefore, although the games are designed to be fun, there is a very serious side to it all. First, learning that a key communicative factor (both expressive and receptive) is facial expression and the use of eyes; secondly, that the range and dimension of a spoken message can change depending on whether you look at the speaker; and thirdly, looking at another's face can be more fun than you think!

Explain how looking at someone's face can be less intimidating if you know some basic mainstream rules for our culture (i.e. there are cultural differences within our own culture, and between different overseas cultures – e.g. more eye-avoidance in Japan than UK, direct eye contact can be more intimidating for some individuals in some UK ethnic groups). Therefore, understanding basic eye-contact rules for the UK can help individuals with weak face-reading skills, and individuals from groups trying to understand, or cope better, with people looking at them. The most unhelpful rule is – look at someone when they are talking to you. Well, OK, I have been saying this already – but only in terms of receiving information. When sending a facial or eye expression at the same time as looking at somebody who is communicating with you, it is best to be aware of the following guidelines.

- **The four second rule** – if you look at someone else's eyes for four seconds or more, it can send a signal that you are beginning to stare at them. This does not mean you should stop looking at them after four seconds. It is a guide for those who may only look into the speaker's eyes. A better approach is to learn the 'soft eye focus' (SEF). SEF is a useful technique for maintaining eye contact, indicating interest, and helping others to feel more comfortable with you (see diagram 2).

Diagram 2: The SEF area

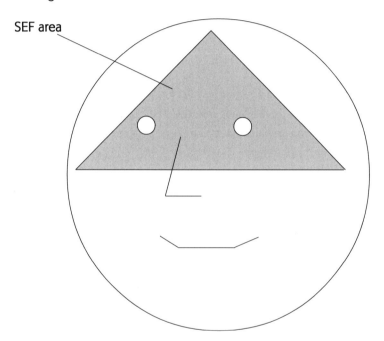

SEF area

The SEF area is an area covering from slightly below the eyes, across the bridge of the nose, forming an upward triangle to the top of the forehead. The SEF technique allows you to look inside that area during a conversation without having to worry about the four-second rule. Of course, looking away is allowed! However, skilled listeners automatically scan the SEF area when someone is communicating with them.

- **The one-second glance rule** – it is usual to glance at strangers when walking in the street, around a supermarket or in a group of people. However, some people take offence, or misinterpret over-long glances, others consider individuals to be surly or untrustworthy if they do not glance at people. A simple rule for looking at strangers is the one-second glance rule, i.e. it is OK to glance for one second and look away – try looking at your group with one-second glances, then two-second glances, then three-second glances. This should show how glances can become stares.

● For further resources on faces and eyes games and exercises, refer to the Appendix at the end of this book.

Posture and gesturing

Postures and gestures can be highly culture-specific. For example, sitting cross-legged with an upturned, flexed foot is a relatively innocent posture in the UK, perhaps indicating interest, boredom, cramp or irritation (depending on other non-verbal clusters). In some regions of south-east Asia it is a gross insult, and can indicate disgust and disdain towards the receiver. Last year, some of the media reported an American who was shot dead while chatting to a local in a Bangkok bar – his only crime: an upward flex of his foot while sitting on a bar stool, which the local man interpreted as 'You are lower than the dirt on the heel of my foot.'

An upturned thumb in the UK indicates 'OK' or 'Can I hitch a lift?' In some regions of China it can be the equivalent of the 'V' sign in the UK. The upright middle finger in the UK is usually interpreted as 'Up yours' – in Cuba it is the equivalent of thumbing a lift, and means 'Room for one only?' A circle formed by the index finger and thumb with three upright fingers is usually interpreted as a sign for 'OK' in western cultures; in some regions of the Middle East it can be interpreted as the 'V' sign's UK equivalent.

These cultural differences can aid conversations with learners when opening the topic on gestures and postures. Indeed, it can alert individuals that different cultures can have different **spoken** languages and different **postural** languages. However, several gestures tend to be universal for most regions of the world, e.g. a nod of the head usually means 'yes', a shake of the head, 'no', foot tapping signalling nervousness or irritation, crossed arms on chest indicating defensiveness or resistance to another's communication.

Many personalities appearing in the British media have modified their postures and gestures to present themselves in a more positive light to their audience. Ten years ago, Tony Blair's speeches were often punctuated with head forward, pointing gestures. He assumed a more open, less aggressive posture by standing upright, with open palms and using both hands turned in towards himself while speaking. So much so, they have now become his trademark with impersonators.

The more aware we become of how postures and gestures affect our communications on others, the greater the likelihood that people's feedback to us will be positive. Often individuals use rejecting signals when they want to be accepted, and it is those types of behaviours that should be coached with positive alternatives.

Guidelines for helping young people to develop better gesturing skills

- Use videotapes of exaggerated gestures (films, TV, home videos) to observe and discuss different meanings for gestures.

- Observe and discuss different emotional states that people may be feeling because of the gestures they are using – this can be direct 'live' observations and/or use of videotape.

- Guess the relationship characters may have with each other, based on the type of gestures used.

- Video the learner with peers and then both of you watch the gestures used, and discuss what they mean, and positive alternatives that may help the learner.

- If possible, acquire tapes of a mime artist – often young people without an understanding of gestures are unable to understand what mime artists are doing. It can be of great benefit to help them understand what the artist is saying non-verbally.

- Produce a pictionary of gestures, gleaned from photographs, print-outs, magazines, etc. Get your learner to help you collect new gestures (including those from other cultures).

- Talk to each other, but only in gestures. Perhaps have cards that can be picked from a pack, each card having a topic that the person has to 'talk' (gesticulate) about e.g. *'How do you feel today?', 'What is your timetable for the day?', 'How do you feel about the weather today?'*

- Play charades – use cards with anger, boredom, fear, sadness, surprise, happiness, confused, etc. Have 'send' and 'receive' cards, i.e. send a sadness gesture – how do you receive the gesture and send one back?

- Exchange 'greetings' gestures: there is not only the nod of the head or handshake – but there are also now many different types of greetings with hands. There is the light touching of knuckles; the handshake with thumbs then interlocking; and the 'fives', when open palms hit each other – footballers do it after scoring a goal (I prefer that to their previous kissing...!); light knuckle touch with clenched hand on top then below the hand of the receiver. Ask the learner whether they know of others, and when each one is OK to use, and with whom. Handshakes can communicate a lot about a person or their intent. Many people still believe a good handshake is a very firm handshake – that might be the case for sport or business. For everyday purposed, a guideline for the learner is: look in the SEF area of the receiver, smile and offer your hand for a handshake, and when hands are shook, hold the other person's hand (like operating a door handle, not like squeezing an empty can, or having a hand like a wet fish). The handshake should convey 'I'm happy to meet you and I can be trusted,' not 'I'm in charge here, and feel the power!'.

Guidelines for helping young people to develop better posturing skills

- Advise your learner that posture conveys something about your attitude, your level of awareness or feelings, e.g. the way you sit or stand.

- Work together on **resting posture**, i.e. 'at ease' in a chair or standing, avoiding 'the slouch'.

- Work together on **active posture**, i.e. leaning forward in chair indicates showing interest; sitting up in chair with both feet flat on floor shows alertness; sitting back in chair with crossed legs means you're relaxed.

- Discuss **defensiveness posture**, i.e. 'dipped' shoulder when talking (shoulder slightly dipped downwards and standing sideways in conversation); or sitting with both legs and/or shoulder sideways.

- Discuss **aggressive posture**, i.e. standing too close (less than 18 inches away) and leaning forward (when standing or sitting); hands on hips; and arms folded and legs astride.

- Discuss **over-confident postures**, e.g. sitting on tables (both sexes) when chairs available, or sitting astride a chair with chair back into chest (Christine Keeler pose); and sitting with legs wide apart (usually males!).

- Raise awareness of 'gait', i.e. way of walking confidently: shoulders back, not drooped like a victim.

- Let the learner observe others with you, and identify the meanings of various postures. Who gives OK posture signals? Who should you steer clear of?

- Make a pictionary of postures, with labels describing the posture.

- Make videos of your learner, discussing the meaning and interpretations of the postures that are filmed.

- Have silent charade conversations with postures.

- Advise on open and closed gestures – many of these are instinctually rooted into our behavioural repertoires. For example, open palm gestures have their instinctual roots in the display behaviour of 'no hidden weapons'. Historically, the suspicion towards individuals with only the backs of their hands showing is based on an instinct of 'do not trust, they may be hiding something'. Therefore, open posture includes displaying open palms when speaking, not having an object (table) in front when discussing, and walking upright without closed posture, i.e. facing individuals as you walk towards them and not talking to them at a slight angle as if you have more important matters to pursue.

The area of posture and gesture is wide and complex, and has the potential to become more complex than necessary. It is advisable to keep it basic and simple, without adding more sophisticated elements. Remember, some young people are unaware of the gesture and posture signals they send out, others do not understand – or notice – the gestural signals people are sending them. Keep it simple and fun with video feedback.

Section 3
Spatial communication

No, not the extra-terrestrial kind, but it has something to do with space invaders! It is to do with guarding our territory. Again, it is instinctual, but many individuals have real difficulty in appreciating another's space. We can all remember the child at school who stood too close, or the colleague who stands a little closer than is comfortable. There are individuals who use space to intimidate others – these are the people to whom we should say *'Please give me a little more space, you are standing too close to me'.* By not telling some people, they may not learn that their distancing is uncomfortable to you; those who are using close proximity for intimidation learn that you will assert and defend yourself.

So 'having our own space' is important to us. There are two types of 'our own space': there is our territory (such as our home, car or desk) and there is our personal space (the proximity space that we carry around with us). Individuals who have problems defining acceptable and unacceptable personal space for others will display problems with spatial communication.

Distance rules

The distances we stand from each other depend on the nature of the relationship with that person or persons, and the context in which we meet. It is simple to assess individuals' understanding of spatial communication, because in western civilisation the intimate, personal, social and public distancing rules are generally consistent, despite some cultural differences.

Diagram 3: Distance rules

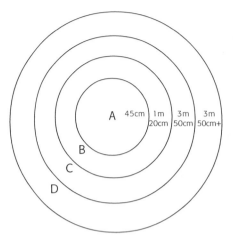

A. Intimate: 45cm or less

B. Personal: 45cm to 1m 20cm

C. Social: 1m 20cm to 3m 50cm

D. Public: more than 3m 50cm

Providing different types of contexts (home, college, work, shopping centre) and different types of relationship (friend or parent, teacher, boss, stranger) to your learner, and asking them appropriate distances to be standing in relation to different situations, you can quickly establish their level of spatial communication skills. It is important to note that in the public zone (over 3m 50cm), there is some awareness of how to communicate before talking, i.e. we would normally be given gestures of some type before engaging in conversation. In other words, verbally greeting someone beyond four metres can cause embarrassment to the receiver. We would normally wait until someone is at a social distance before greeting them verbally.

We do invade others' space on a daily basis, but our acceptance of others on a social level is how we communicate when we, perhaps, lean across a table for something *('Excuse me')* or pick up some item we may have dropped close to somebody's personal space *('Do you mind if I...')*. Not applying these spatial verbal rules can also cause spatial communication problems with others.

Touch

Touch plays a major role in spatial communication. In the UK, we prefer to be touched less than any other country in the world. This can cause major problems. Indeed, despite the British patience for queuing, there is less tolerance of inadvertent touching in queues. Before open-plan cafeterias and restaurants in motorway service stations, there was many a confrontation in queues – especially when coaches arrived (can you similarly elderly types remember the regular signs for 'No coaches'?). Queues, if not providing personal space, can become potentially explosive – especially when the queue is filled with individuals from a country who like being touched the least! Hence, the last 20 years and the success of open-plan shopping malls, self-service restaurants, large stadia, and roomy waiting areas. The tube and the railways have yet to catch up!

So what are the rules in a culture about OK touches, and not-OK touches? Here are some of the *key* rules for individuals to know and learn: if attracting someone's attention when they have their back to you, and you do not know their name, the use of *'Excuse me'* and perhaps a light tap in the *middle or top* of their shoulder is acceptable – we are breaking into someone else's personal space, so we show respect. If we inadvertently move into someone else's space (a trip, or being pushed into that space), *'Sorry'* should follow. These are items to check with your learner when assessing their knowledge of spatial communication. For OK and not-OK silhouette patterns, see diagram 4 (Nowicki and Duke, 1992).

Diagram 4: Silhouette test

Where on this silhouette is it OK to touch a person you do not know intimately? (e.g. an acquaintance, peer, colleague)

Where on this silhouette is it OK to touch people who you know very well? (e.g. parents, brother, sister, girlfriends, boyfriends, husband, wife, etc)

Those individuals who exhibit problems in recognising areas of the body that are not acceptable to touch are displaying spatial communication problems in relation to touch.

- It is generally acceptable to touch *others* on the outside of the bodyline – touching on the inside of the bodyline is emotionally laden (Nowicki and Duke, 1992). This includes the inside of the arms, legs and the sides of the chest.

- Taps, brushing and stroking rules – again, these are restricted to levels of intimacy, context and conveying positive communications.

Strategies and guidelines

Below are listed some strategies and guidelines for helping individuals with spatial communication problems and related difficulties e.g. appropriate touching.

- Use Nowicki's silhouette (see diagram 4) for examining OK and non-OK touches. Ensure that any individuals who are used as an example are placed in several different contexts (e.g. OK touches for mother versus a teacher, OK touches for a friend versus a work colleague, etc).

- Observe individuals with your learner, discussing OK and non-OK touches. What could someone think or feel by someone touching them?

- With permission, touch the learners outside the bodyline and (within ethical bounds!) inside the bodyline. Ask the learner what these different touches may convey.

- Examine intensity of touch, e.g. patting, pushing, etc. – guiding someone with hands on shoulders as opposed to holding their upper arms (one is positive guidance, the other is aggressive direction).

- Provide feedback on what the learner may be telling you on OK touches.

(**NB**: this type of training should only be made with learner's permission, learner's family/parental permission, and permission from your organisation).

Section 4
Non-verbal aspects of speaking

Non-verbal aspects of speaking, sometimes referred to as paralanguage or paralinguistics, include voice volume, voice tone and intonation, the anatomy of 'um' and 'er', and pauses. Some or all of these aspects can convey the emotion of a communication. First, we need to advise our learners on these differing types of communication through words.

Voice volume

The loudness or timidity of someone's voice can isolate them or make them a victim. The use of a neutral tone is useful in different situations – it should become quicker and slightly louder when something amusing is about to be said, slower and more methodical for making important points, and quieter and gentler for showing support or encouragement. The key is understanding when to modify voice volume.

Voice tone and intonation

This is probably best understood by practising the numerous different ways of saying 'yes' or 'no' or 'I hate you' or 'thank you' or 'oh, really'.

The anatomy of 'um' and 'er'

These are the gaps, spaces and hesitations within speech. They can serve the useful purpose of giving yourself more time to think, or deliberately conveying uncertainty over an issue. I often advise young people when on a works placement to use 'um' and 'er' before they answer – it can avoid their being sent back quickly by responding too spontaneously. Also, their use is important for individuals who find it hard to stop expletives flowing freely.

For example:
Dave would use an 'F', 'B' or 'C' word in every sentence he spoke. He isolated himself from many of his peers and teachers. By giving him the option of substituting 'ums' and 'ers' for FBCs **in specific situations** to begin with (e.g. females who were older than him at college), his rate of swearing began to reduce. He was then able to generalise this to other groups.

Activities and techniques

Once aspects of non-verbal speaking are introduced, activities and techniques can be introduced.

- Using audiotape/CD recorder, develop an audio dictionary of voice tones, each representing different emotions and attitudes.

- Without looking at the video/TV screen, let the learner describe the facial expressions, gestures and spatial elements of actors they listen to on screen. Play back the video to see how well they have performed.

- Say the same sentence five times. Ask the learner what each sentence conveys, e.g. happiness, sadness, anger, interest, fear.

- Play voice tone charades – the friendly conversation, the grumpy conversation, the angry conversation, the neutral conversation (providing information not emotion).

- Read a passage from a book and change the emotional voice tone, and ask the learner to shout out what is the new voice tone.

- Use answerphones for learners to leave messages in:

  - a formal tone (asking for an application form, making an appointment, etc)

- an informal tone (leaving a message for a friend about meeting that night, leaving a message for a relation about the time they will be home, etc)

- a neutral tone (leaving information for a colleague).

- Use a grading system for your learner when interacting with peers, teachers, employers, visitors, etc. For example, when visitors arrive, I often ask one of my clients to meet them. My client will appreciate that I will ask the visitor how they got along. I will ask the visitor to grade my client on a scale of A to E on voice tone, social distancing, touch (perhaps there was a handshake), facial expression, and eye contact. I will report back to the client how the visitor graded them.

References

Baron-Cohen, S. (1989), *The Autistic Child's Theory of Mind: a Case of Specific Developmental Delay*, Journal of Child Psychology and Psychiatry, **10** (2), 285-297.

Baron-Cohen, S. and Jolliffe, T. (1997), *Another Advanced Test of Theory of Mind: Evidence from Very High Functioning Adults with Autism or Aspergers Syndrome*, Journal of Child Psychology and Psychiatry, **38**(7), 813-822.

Bruno, R. (1981), *Interpretation of Pictorially Presented Situations by Learning Disabled and Normal Children*, Journal of Learning Disabilities, **14**, 350-2.

Crick, N.R. and Dodge, K.A. (1994), *A Review and Reformulation of Social Information Processing Mechanisms in Children's Social Adjustment*, Psychological Bulletin, **115**(1), 74-101.

Dimitrovski, L., Spector, H., Levy-Shiff, R. and Vakil, E. (1998), *Interpretation of facial expressions of affect in children with learning disabilities with verbal or non-verbal deficits*, Journal of Learning Disabilities, **28**(5), 286-292.

Dodge, K.A., Asher, S.R. and Parkhurst, J.T. (1989), *Social life as a Goal Coordination Task* in C. Ames and R. Ames (Eds) *Research on Motivation in Education* (Volume 3), London: Academic Press.

Farrington, D.P. (1991), *Antisocial Personality from Childhood to Adulthood,* The Psychologist, **4**(9), 389-394.

Fawcett, A. (2001), *Dyslexia: Theory and Good Practice*, London: Whurr Publishers.

Happé, F. (1999), *Understanding Assets and Deficits in Autism: Why Success Is More Interesting Than Failure*, The Psychologist, **12**(11), 540-546.

Hobson, R.P., Ouston, J. and Lee, T. (1988), *What's in a Face?*, British Journal of Psychology, **79**, 441-453.

Irlen, H.(1991), *Scotopic Sensitivity Syndrome – Screening Manual*, Long Beach, CA: Perceptual Development Corporation.

Kinsbourne, M.(1991), *Overfocusing: an Apparent Subtype of ADHD*, in N.Amir, I.Rapin, and D. Branski (Eds) *Pediatric neurology: Behaviour and Cognition of the Child with Brain Damage* (Volume 1). Basel: Karger.

Kuhne, M. and Weiner, J. (2000), *Stability of Social Status of Children With and Without Learning Disabilities,* Learning Disability Quarterly, **23**(1), 64-75.

Lamb, E. and Joshi, M.S. (2002), *Michael Argyle*, The Psychologist, **15**(12), 624-5.

Lombard, G.F. (1992), *Enhancing Adolescents' Self-Efficacy Through the Application of a Social-Cognitive Motivational Approach*, PhD Thesis, University of Bristol Library.

Lombard, G.F. (2003), *More Social Competency Games*, Swindon: Wakefield Publications.

Lombard, G.F. and Bigglestone, A. (2002), *A Study of Soft Skills Training with Training Providers in South East Wales*, Cardiff: ELWa (Education and Learning Wales).

Lombard, G.F. and Bigglestone, A. (2003), *Life Skills in Lancashire*, Lancashire: The Independent Psychological Service/LSC.

Lombard, G.F., Barrett, J.H.W. and Mason, L. (2003), *Assessments to Measure Social Competencies*, Swindon: Wakefield Publications.

Nowicki, S. and Duke, M. (1992), *Helping The Child Who Doesn't Fit In*, Atlanta, GA: Peachtree Press.

Nowicki, S. and Duke, M. (2002), *Will I Ever Fit In?* New York: Free Press.

Parker, J. and Asher, S.R. (1987), *Peer Acceptance and Later Personal Adjustment: Are Low Accepted Children at Risk?* Psychological Bulletin, **102**, 357-389.

Pemberton, A. (1999), *Looking at Autism,* Irlen Institute Internal Newsletter, **10**(2), 5.

Piven, J., Arndt, S., Bailey, J., Havercamp, S., Anderson, N.C. and Palmer, P. (1995), *An MRI Study of Brain Size in Autism*, American Journal of Psychiatry, **152**, 1145-9.

Rourke, B.P. and Fuerst, D.R. (1991), Learning Disabilities and Psychosocial Functioning: A Neurological Perspective, New York: Guilford.

Stafford, C.S. and Grosser, G.S. (1993), *The Social Misperception Syndrome in Children with Learning Disabilities: Social Causes Versus Neurological Variables*, Journal of Learning Disabilities, **26**(3), 178-189, 198.

Tracey, D.K. and Gleeson, G. (1998) *Self-reported Social and Personal Experiences of Adolescents with ADHD*, The Australian Educational and Developmental Psychologist, **15**(1), 23-33.

Whiting, P.R. and Robinson, G.L. (2002), *The Interpretation of Emotion from Facial Expression*, paper presented at VII International Irlen Conference, Vancouver, 11-14 July 2002.

Appendix

Assessments and programmes

This booklet has been designed as a basic introduction to the area of social competency. Fortunately, there are now assessments, games and programmes available from a variety of sources to further extend social competency training. Often, these resources are suitable for children, teenagers and adults. Below are recommended resources for developing further social competency training programmes.

The DANVA2 (Nowicki and Duke, 2002)

A CD-ROM and booklet that can be used both as an assessment tool and teaching package. It focuses upon facial expression and emotional tone of voice. It is from USA, and voices on the CD have American accents. It is a good introduction to face and voice recognition. Available from: Dyssemia Inc., 260 Weatherly Drive, Fayetteville, GA 30214 – 1790, USA.

Social Competence Assessments (Lombard, Barrett and Mason, 2003)

A series of four assessments to determine:

- reading of eyes (expressions)

- coping styles

- levels of aspiration

- planning vs impulsive strategists.

Assessments are available individually, or can be bought together. Available from: Wakefield Publications, 54 Kent Road, Swindon SN1 3NG.

The Social Skills Game (Streng and Searle, 1996)

An excellent combination of game and activities to provoke humour in the learning of social competences. Highly recommended. Available from: Jessica Kingsley Publishers, 116 Pentonville Road, London N1 9JB.

Mind Reading (2003) DVD-ROM and CD-ROM

Developed by Simon Baron-Cohen, University of Cambridge. Contact: www.human-emotions.com

More Social Competency Games (Lombard, 2003)

More activities and games to encourage social play and understanding the importance of social skills and reading others' behaviour. Available from: Wakefield Publications, 54 Kent Road, Swindon SN1 3NG.